FROM ACE
TO ZOWIE

FROM ACE TO ZOWIE

THE ULTIMATE GUIDE TO HIP BABY NAMES

Tobias Anthony

Smith
Street
Books

THE MODERN HIPSTER IS GROWING UP.

Well, let's call it a transitional period. They're leaving their twenties behind and entering their thirties. They're moving out of the scary neighbourhoods and into the gentrified ones. They're settling down, which means less time spent in bars and more time spent browsing their local artisanal markets. But perhaps most frightening of all – O! Cruel passage of time! – they're even thinking about ... having children.

This book has been put together to help hipsters with busy lives brainstorm the perfect names for their future world-changers and trendsetters. We have taken care to factor in the limited time available to the average hipster, who is typically stretched thin between curating multiple social media accounts, distilling whiskey, building terrariums and gathering yarn for the next act of guerrilla knitting, not to mention the hour spent each day queuing for the trendiest food truck. Choosing a name for a baby is hard, but the hardest thing of all is coming to the difficult realisation that the name you choose is a permanent decision, and not something that can be undone (at least, not until the child turns eighteen).

So here's our guide. We're here to help. This is our list of some names we hope will never go away.

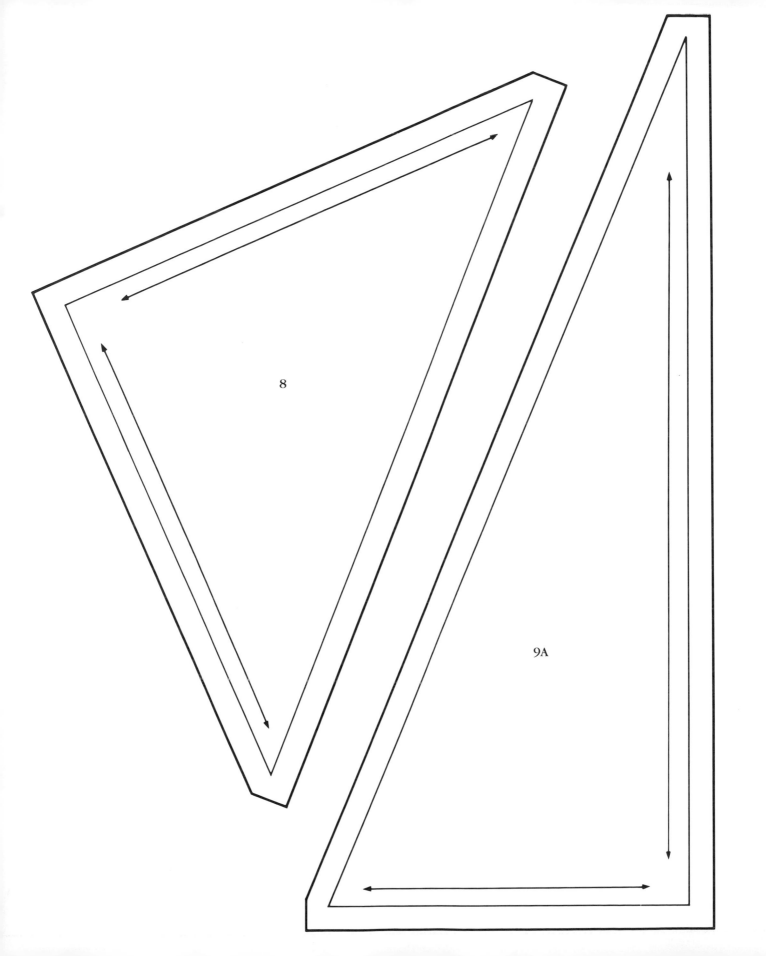

Ace

You can't beat this one. Or so people who know
nothing about cards will tell you.

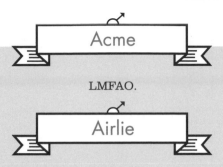

Acme

LMFAO.

Airlie

It might mean 'promise'; it might mean 'eagle wood'. Who knows? Who even cares? Airy-fairy, much?

Ajax

The roots of this name extend to Greek mythology, but this might be one case in which a Greek warrior is defeated by a household cleaner.

Alden

Perfect for both boys and girls, Alden is derived from an Old English surname meaning 'old friend'. How lovely.

Alessandro

There isn't a bigger hipster in the world than Italy's tattooed silver fox, Alessandro Manfredini. And if you're following this bearded legend on Instagram, then congratulations: you might just be the second biggest hipster in the world.

Anest
♀

Split the name into two and you have a house for birds. Everyone likes birds.

Apollo
♂

Obviously a Greek mythology name, though you could take a different route when explaining your decision to grant your son this name. How about the Apollo Theatre in Harlem, NYC? Performers who have graced this stage include Ray Charles, Duke Ellington, Buddy Holly, Louis Armstrong, and the Jackson 5.

Archie
♂

Meaning 'truly brave', you don't have to be to choose this one, with its pleasantly retro sound. *Archie* comics are dead and so too is the actor who played Archie Bunker on the 1970s sitcom *All in the Family*. So go ahead and follow the lead of one of the coolest mothers in showbiz, Amy Poehler, whose first son bears this name.

Ari
♂

Here's a sentence: 'Ari's jeans were so tight that he had to be cut out of them.' Now, tell me that hasn't happened to you at least once while shopping.

Arlo
♂

So Arlo was never quite the sensation his father, Woody Guthrie, was, but like you Arlo liked to bitch and moan about social injustice. Only, unlike you, he had some real beefs: stuff like war and nuclear power, not how annoying (and possibly racist) it is that major supermarket chains don't sell kimchi.

Astara

Sure, it's a city in Iran – or 'Persia' if you're explaining this to hawkish friends –
but it also sounds lovely, yes?

Atlas

Yes, it's true: you *do* have the greatest social conscience the world has ever known.
But it must be a heavy load you're carrying. Perhaps it's time to pass the burden
onto someone else and let them take up the slacktivism.

Atticus

A perfect name for a young lad that will let your friends know you've read a few
books. Just don't mention that other one she wrote.

Aubrey

If you're expecting a particularly short (or tall) boy or girl, you might want to
consider this name, which means 'elf ruler' in Old German.

Auden

This name actually means 'old friend'. Kind of endearing, no? And don't forget
that famous poet, either.

August

Meaning 'majestic' and 'venerable', August is absolutely everything those Buzzfeed articles you're reading are not.

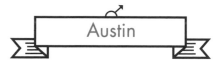

Austin

This is another one that peaked in popularity during the 1990s, and we all know what that means. That's right, time to bring it back.

Avant

Here's a name that paints a picture: experimental, innovative, culturally and stylistically advanced, French. *Dang!* Nothing screams chic this loudly.

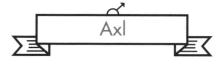

Axl

Mmm, yes … I can see him now, fully grown: hair slicked back, bearded, wearing a denim jacket and waxing lyrical about the rockabilly lifestyle.

Azalea

In the words of her namesake, Iggy: 'Drop this and let the whole world feel it.' Fancy!

Banksy

A lifetime of graffitied walls and never really getting to know your son awaits you, but who cares? He'll be raking in millions.

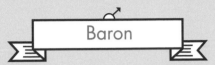

Baron

Donald Trump has a son named Barron, although he chose to spell it with two Rs. Still, this one has been tarnished.

Bear

All I can see is Bear Grylls stuffing his face full of insects while drinking his own urine. Come on, guys, you can't name your child after their favourite toy – that's just a basic rule to live by. *I wonder why Furby didn't make it onto this list?*

Beat

You're gravitating towards this because of its literary connotations, but I can see right through you. You've only read *On The Road*. And face it, it's kind of the only good one out of the lot.

Beatrix

Along with that hipster cred–earning X, this one is derived from Latin and means 'she who brings happiness'. (It's the old-school version of 'she whose milkshake brings all the boys to the yard'.)

Beryl

Hitting the height of its popularity around 1910 when, inexplicably, it was also a reasonably popular boy's name, Beryl refers to a sea-green gem. Totes masculine.

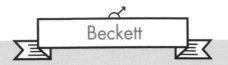

Beckett

If you weren't utterly confused and/or bored while studying the playwright in whichever tertiary course you took, then go right ahead. But do you really want a son digging the modernists?

Beethoven

Let's hope this one falls on deaf ears. Just saying.

Benji

Permanent nicknames are bold and they demonstrate a confidence on the part of the name-giver, although nothing can compete with the statement Benji's future man-bun will make.

Bento

My childhood was spent feeling lonely and bored during church services and piano lessons I was forced to attend. Long dinners in Japanese restaurants might replace both those things for your progeny.

Blair

It rhymes with flair, which your boy is bound to have in abundance. He's an individual, don't you know? He's a star!

Blaire

Derived from a Scottish surname with the somewhat, well, *plain* meaning of 'dweller on the plain'. Of course, there are advantages to living somewhere unencumbered by hills – it's an easy ride on your fixie.

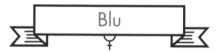

Blaize

If you think your child is likely to have a speech impediment, best avoid this name, which is Latin for 'lisp, stutter'. Still, the 'z' in it is pretty great, yes?

Blu

Drop the last letter off of any colour and it spells ... well, something else that reminds you of that original word only ... like, um ... misspelled? Sorry, I think I might've messed this one up.

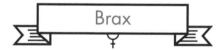

Brax

She's the daughter of Drax The Destroyer. You know, from that cool, fun film starring the blonde guy from that cool, fun show. You know, pop culture, right?

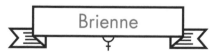

Brienne

This Celtic-derived name meaning 'high, noble, exalted' is the feminine version of Brian. *Yawn*. It's also the name of a character in *Game of Thrones*. Unyawn!

Brogues

Alternatively, you could always try Brogan on for size, but I'm not sure how this one makes the grade, really. You're wearing New Balance trainers, not cow hide.

Brooklyn

Do you find yourself with a wardrobe filled with jackets from The North Face? Have you ever worn a beanie on a hot day? Do you like Reuben sandwiches and cold-brew coffee? Of course you do. Your son's name is Brooklyn, after all.

Bryn

One to avoid if you reside in Wales, where this boys' name for 'hill' is as common as John. But no hipsters reside in Wales anyway, right?

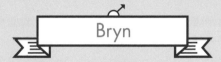
Burlap

Do you want an ugly baby? Because this is how you get an ugly baby.

Butch

Are you sure this isn't too macho for an infant? This is a baby name book, you realise. I dunno, maybe Butch goes perfectly in the crib nestled beside twin sister Spike. Aww, now that's adorable.

Byron

Meaning 'barn for cows' ... No? Still with me? Okay, well it was also James Dean's middle name and who else do you refer to when you're choosing your next hair cut?

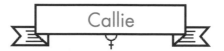

Callie

While it sounds a little like boring old Kelly, the Hellenic roots of this name – Greek for 'most beautiful' – give it the double hipster whammy of being obnoxiously superlative *and* obnoxiously European.

Callisto

A name derived from ancient Greek, Callisto was a nymph who transformed into a bear and hung out among the stars. Yup, sure. It's also the name of one of Jupiter's cooler moons.

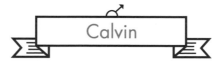

Calvin

Possibly even worse than Byron above, Calvin actually means 'bald'. So, yeah ...

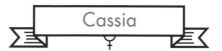

Cassia

The feminine form of Cassius, and it's a tree! The Cassia tree produces beautiful yellow flowers and a spice that can be used to replace cinnamon. So don't call your baby girl Cinnamon like a douche.

Caulfield

One day they'll write articles about this young man and his brave decision to quit social media. The tears are welling up already.

Cecily

An old lady name – derived from the Latin for 'dim-sighted' – that is seeing some modern resurgence, much like macramé and growing enormous beards.

Chester

Ah, Chester. You've got to love the anaemic little bastard, always quaffing organic green juices and stuffing his mouth full of vegan cookies. It's just too bad all those life hacks you read about never prepared you for this level of disappointment.

Chia

Just like those tiny black seeds you sprinkle into your protein smoothie. But save this name for your third child, the sibling of Wheatgrass and Goji. Hot tip, BTW: save Spirulina for child number four.

Chopan

The name of a small town in India. Cool, I guess ... Possibly the place you discovered *that* side of yourself. You know, the other side that you couldn't find in South America.

Clive

Derived from a surname meaning 'cliff' in Old English, the original Clive was somebody who lived near a cliff. How boring. But Clive has had a rich history. At some point he was wearing a pith helmet and a pencil-thin moustache, digging trenches and colonising continents. Most recently he's been a rather masculine British actor who might've made a good Bond. Give Clive a chance.

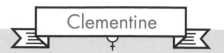

Clementine

Immortalised in that terrible earworm from the late nineteenth century, 'Oh My Darling...', this is one name (and citrus fruit) that has endured. French in origin, this name has modern celeb cred, thanks to the daughter of Ethan Hawke.

Cleo

An abbreviation of the name of one of history's most powerful women, Cleo has a touch of class with that rounded 'o' sound at the end. Just roll it around your mouth a couple of times; don't you just want to say it over and over?

Clover

The meaning of this name in Anglo-Saxon is ... 'clover'. Well, at least that's easy to remember. Fun fact: Angelina Jolie played a Clover once, in a film starring Matt Damon and directed by Robert de Niro. Impressive, no? Not really: it got, like, a 54 on Rotten Tomatoes.

Collette

A name lost for decades, Collette is seeing a rise in popularity. And why not? After all, every party needs a Collette. *I'm hells jeal of how gorgeous Collette's new neck tattoo is.'*

Colton

Colton is a born trendsetter with his smooth, two-syllable name. Now all he has to do is master the many ways one can tie a scarf.

Copernicus

'Copernicus! Copernicus! Copernicus!' they chanted.

Cormac

This one calls to mind another literary great and it's a happy-sounding name too, don't you think? Just remember that *The Road* is not an uplifting tale of father-son bonding.

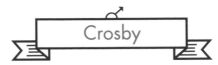

Crosby

If Stills and Nash aren't on your radar, then don't let Crosby fall off your list, too. Say it a few times and give this name a chance: it's got a real zippy zing to it. That said, let's hope nobody confuses this with Cosby. Bill has kind of gone and destroyed that one now, hasn't he?

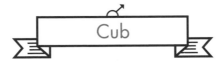

Cub

Like Fox, which you will come across if you flip ahead, I don't mind this one. Although, unlike Fox, I can't really see anybody graduating into adulthood under the moniker. It's a name that is permanently babyish and I'm not certain we'll ever get past that. What chance does Cub stand integrating with the menfolk?

Daisy

Ah, isn't this one lovely? *Daisy, Daisy, Daisy. How my heart yearns for thee.* Oh, right, *baby* names.

Dali

Surrealism is all fun and games until little Dali slices your eyeball open with a straight razor.

Dashiell

There are only two things that can make Dashiell cry: spilt almond milk and the knowledge that other people know the name of his favourite band.

Datsun

A brand of car owned by Nissan, Datsuns were phased out in 1986. Which means it's just about revival time.

Dax

We're rolling two hipster favourites into one here: a monosyllabic name with the letter X! Best to avoid if you're an Aussie, however. In Australia, the homonym 'dacks' means underwear.

Deck

You might have been attracted to the name Declan, but Deck is the new Declan, didn't you know? But if you're worried people won't take this one too seriously, just tell them you were inspired by the Felicia Hemans poem written in 1826. That'll shut them down!

Delilah

My, my, my. Is there anyone cooler than Tom Jones? I think not. This name has inspired a few songs – Florence and the Machine have a 'Delilah' of their own, don't you know? (Silly question – of course you do!) – and with good reason, too. In Hebrew the name means 'amorous', 'delight', 'languishing' and 'temptress'.

Delphine

The more feminine and French (ooh la la!) form of the Greek name Delphina, this name guarantees little Delphie will grow up to sport kaftans.

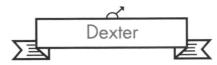

Dexter

So what if your boy's namesake was a loveable serial killer from TV? Hijacking pop culture for your own ends is what you do. It's why places like Cereal Killer Café exist.

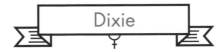

Diner

For the retro enthusiasts out there, this name provides a helping of nostalgia – can't you just hear the jukebox and taste the sweet soda pop? A twist on the name Dinah, meaning 'avenged', 'judged and vindicated'.

Dixie

Another X – and we love those, don't we? Dixie is bursting at the seams with pop cultural relevance: there's a female wrestler, an actress, a band, an entire genre of music and, in Australia, even ice cream. Still not enough? Then follow the lead of Kings of Leon frontman Caleb Followill: his daughter's name is Dixie.

Django

Every accessory needs a name and Django is the perfect option for the little boy you dress in plaid trousers and waltz about vintage clothing stores.

Dreya

Aerial silk is a type of performance in which one or more artists perform aerial acrobatics while hanging from a special fabric. And you know who does this? Dreya Weber, that's who. Okay, so I've got nothing. But you should look up Dreya Weber. Seriously. She has worked with Madonna and Pink and Cher and she describes herself as omniscxual. I don't even know what that means!

Dries

'Dries, my boy, come and sit on daddy's knee. I have something to show you.' 'What is it?' 'Why, Dries, this is called a typewriter.' 'What does it do?' 'Well, it types up words, silly.' 'But why do we have this when we have a computer?' 'Because we're daft, Dries. We're really, very daft.'

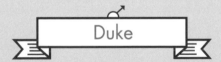
Duke

What's more retro than a good old-fashioned western flick? This name calls to mind John Wayne's nickname. The Duke, of course, was anti-Communism and pro the Vietnam War, so good luck explaining this one to your friends.

Dunham

Ever watched that show *Girls*? Of course you have.

♀

Elna

This is a variation on the name Eleanor (and
you are so right not to name your child Eleanor,
BTW) and it is also a ... brand of sewing machine.
I guess this works too, because [insert joke about
yarn bombing].

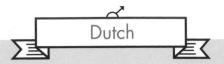

Dutch

Fond of farting? Yes? Your child's name should certainly be an ode to the time you trapped your partner under the sheets, then.

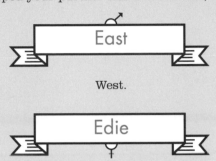

East

West.

Edie

You loved that course on postmodernism and you came to worship Andy and his cans of soup. So why not name your daughter after his favourite 'It Girl'?

Edison

Is this winding the clock back too far, or not far enough? It's old-school, that's for sure. And I get the feeling that in some steampunk alternate world Edison kind of became like what John is to us today.

Elvis

No, no, no. Don't bring this one back. We don't need this one.

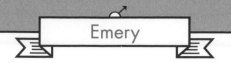

Emery

Meaning 'industrious', this one is typically a female name, but don't let that stop you. Someone has to break down these stifling barriers dictating what is and isn't 'normal'.

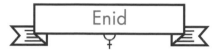

Enid

Can you say retro? If so, then Enid fits in with some other words that spring to mind: cardigan, horn-rimmed, Sunday roast. Now that I think about it, is this such a good idea?

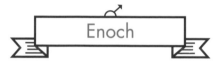

Enoch

I know you. I know the type. It wasn't enough to own a fixie, was it? No, you had to go out and buy a penny-farthing. Well, in the spirit of one-upmanship, Enoch is the name for you.

Ernestine

If you're considering this name unironically, then whatever you do please don't – I repeat, please *do not* – Google 'Lily Tomlin + Ernestine'.

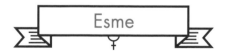

Esme

If you were living in sixteenth century Scotland right now, this would be a man's name. But you're not, so don't worry. This name originates from the French meaning 'esteemed' or 'loved'. Pretty fancy, which is probably why celebs Michael J Fox, Samantha Morton and Katey Sagal have all chosen the name for their offspring.

Esmeralda

She's a friend o' hunchbacks *and* her name is Greek for 'emerald'; what's not to like?

Ethel

There's not a name more noble, which is what it means in Old English. Don't be put off by the misery that surrounds this moniker; Ethel isn't just the name of Robert Kennedy's widow or that famous atomic spy executed in 1953. It's also the name of Lily Allen's daughter. So smile!

Etta

You're a hipster, which means you have to stay ahead of the curve. Leave Emma and Ella behind and follow the march of progress, just like you did when you moved into that newly gentrified neighbourhood.

Everly

Oh Everly, how I wish that I could endorse you. But you just don't make any goddamned sense. Which is cool, actually, now that I think about it. It's kind of like one of those Tim and Eric sketches.

Eyelet

Make up your own mind. I'm leaving this one alone.

Fallon

Really? Okay, I'll try, but this one just seems like a bad omen. It's slick, I guess. But I can't stop myself from imagining a blonde teen from 1980s Los Angeles. Who is a boy. Who deals coke. Sorry.

Farron

This one actually means 'handsome servant', but that's etymology, not a job description.

Fedora

Your favourite hat is now your daughter's name ... Yeah, maybe think this one through.

Felix

Most people might think of the cat and assume this is one of those names more pet than person, but this is a really happy sounding name, which is kind of what it means. And don't forget the character Felix Unger, either.

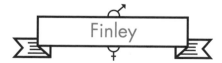

Finley

Good for either boy or girl, Finley means 'fair-haired hero', which seems a little, I dunno ... racist? Time to reclaim this one, ladies and gentlemen, and make the kind of statement your fair-trade coffee can't.

Finn

Yeah, sure, it's only got one syllable. But if you were really with it you would've dropped that second N.

Fixie

I think the word you're looking for is 'zeitgeist'. Actually, is there room in the Zs for another name?

Fleetwood

There's nothing to say here except Stevie Nicks is a goddess and everybody should know you listen to a vinyl copy of *Tusk* on the reg.

Flora

The name of the Roman goddess of flowers and spring, it's another flower name meaning flower. Isn't that nice? Alternatively, you could opt for Fleur. So there you go, that's a free bonus name idea.

Folk

Meaning at once 'people', 'chief' and 'army' or 'legion' in Old Norse, this name will provide you with hours of fun trying to choose what kind of Viking you'd like your child to be. Yay for whimsy. Yay for choice.

♂

Fox

I've got to say, I've warmed to this one. While
it's a very simple name, it manages to evoke a
certain sleekness balanced with an untamed,
unruly, animal … *thing*. I don't know. I like it.
I want to believe.

Frances

A classic name with a long history and one that provides several nicknames, including Frankie, Fran and Fanny (just don't use this one in Australia or the UK – or the States, come to think of it). And did you know that Judy Garland's real name was Frances Ethel Gumm? I can't imagine why she would change it.

Frank

Really? We're bringing this back? Your call, I guess. But I tend to prefer names that don't sound like a person bringing up phlegm.

Frankie

A nickname for Frances, Frankie retains the meaning of that name, which is 'free'. Doesn't that just make your liberated heart melt?

Freddy

There's so much pop culture here that I don't know where to start. Secretly, I just hope you guys will make names taken from horror movie monsters a thing. Imagine getting Freddy, Jason and Godzilla all ready for school in the morning. Now there's an image of a happy family.

Freya

I dated a girl named Lee once and she wore Lee jeans and thought this was cool. Your Freya may do likewise, only with Freya lingerie and swimwear. It's a brand, trust me. In Old Norse Frejya means 'lady', so it's a perfect name for a girl.

Gage

Meaning 'oath' or 'pledge', Gage is flexible with the spelling. Try also Gaige and/or Gauge. Wow, so much choice. It's like shopping on Etsy, isn't it?

Gimlet

An ideal name for a hipster bub, as a gimlet is also a popular Jazz-age cocktail made from gin and lime. Just be sure to name your cat Gatsby.

Godric

'Godric's Tumblr posts were the stuff of legends,' they'll say. This is, of course, after he takes a dive off the tallest building in town. An Old English name that was last popular before the Norman conquest, it popped up once more in JK Rowling's *Harry Potter* series, which you already know, of course.

Gracie

What happens when you take the nickname of Grace (which means 'divine grace', of course) and place it as the official name on your child's birth certificate? Well, according to some nut on the Internet, you end up with a girl who befriends tall people, is often found skipping around happily, and has a fondness for green jello. The Internet, everybody.

Graff

Street art might be your life and your passion, but now I'm wondering whether the fumes might have caused some permanent damage.

Gryff

Do you know what a yoga rave is? Yes? Then go ahead and name your child Gryff.

Gulliver

There isn't a continent you haven't set foot in and you need everyone to know just what travelling means to you. (Yes, we know, it's more than simply buying an aeroplane ticket and physically being in a new location.) Go ahead, inflict that wisdom you've accumulated over the years on your child.

Gus

This sounds like the perfect name for somebody who will grow up drinking out of mason jars and spending their Saturdays learning rustic crafts.

Gyoza

See Bento. One day, we're going to be consoling ourselves with sushi and telling our children that we're sorry, but we think we might have broken a system that worked.

Hamlet

Do everybody involved a favour and just pull the trigger on this name.

Hank

The diminutive of Henry, Hank surprisingly means 'estate ruler'. But was Hank ever a baby? This name only seems fit for a baby boy whose testicles have already dropped by the time he has left the womb.

Harley

You're not going to name your son after a motorbike, not with all that terrible pollution they produce. Try Fixie instead.

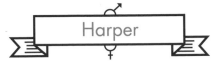

Harper

A unisex name, Harper remains a unique choice for a baby girl. But why should it be? It's a strong and original name that happens to mean 'harpist'. But surely I shouldn't need to convince you that it's feminine enough – not with your unmatched open-mindedness.

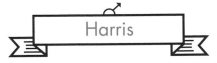

Harris

Harry is boring and Harrison is a bridge too far. So why not meet somewhere in the middle? This name teaches an important life lesson: compromise.

Hazel

Get over that image you have of your arthritic great-aunt slopping gravy on her mashed taters. And forget those sounds she made slurping it up off her spoon after removing her false teeth. Hazel is modern now. She's the protagonist of smash-hit book (and film) *The Fault in our Stars*. Don't you have a heart?

Henning

If you actually know who Doug Henning is, then you truly are a hipster wunderkind. Nothing says 'obscure retro bullshit' quite like referencing a Canadian magician from the 1970s.

Hermione

You came of age reading books about wizards, then you left high school and got yourself some geometric tattoos. Why are you even considering anything else?

Holden

The obvious literary connection here is to J D Salinger's beloved coming-of-age novel, *The Catcher in the Rye*. But this traditional English name also manages to hold its own, meaning 'from the hollow in the valley'.

Homer

We might be past the point of *Simpsons* relevance, but you should be slapping yourself on the forehead and screaming 'D'oh!' if you really though this one would make it past the goalie.

Hopper

Whether you like insane American actors who pop up in Lynch movies to inhale gas, chew blue velvet and dry-hump Italian women, or whether you're just a really big fan of kangaroos, this name's got you covered.

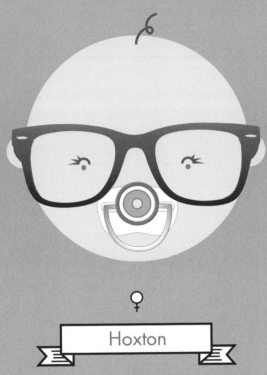

♀

Hoxton

This isn't a name, it's a London hipster hotspot,
which is why it's in here. That's kinda the point
of this, right?

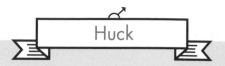

Huck

If you liked Duke, then this could be another option for you – but I'm against putting down the short form of Huckleberry on a birth certificate. You never know; one day your boy might appreciate being able to reveal his full name at parties.

Hudson

This one packs a manly punch. Famous namesakes include heartthrob actor Rock Hudson and English explorer Henry Hudson, as well as the Hudson River, which travels through that hippest of hipster cities, New York.

Hugo

Could you please explain what there is to like about this one? It sounds doltish to me, which is ironic seeing as one of its meanings is actually 'intellect'.

Hunter

Yes, this is a rugged one, isn't it? But if young Hunter can't participate in contact sports, he's going to seem rather foolish. After all, his namesake, Hunter S Thompson – and don't try to deny this isn't his namesake either – epitomised many a manly pursuit, including playing football and shooting firearms.

Icarus

Where bad omens are concerned, this one has to take the cake. But forgetting the mythology for a moment, this makes for a curious name choice – it's got just the right amount of snappiness to help a young lad build his social media profile sky high.

Ike

Don't kick the goddamn baby!

India

This name was first made popular in England during the British rule of India in the nineteenth century, and we all know what a happy time that was. But the name has seen increased popularity in recent years and makes for a lovely reminder (besides enlightenment, of course) of your ashram days.

Indiana

This one could be given to a boy or a girl – just don't let your kid dress up like Indiana Jones. Recently some interstate friends visited with their son, and he wore the outfit for the entire four days: hat, whip, everything. Kids in costumes are creepy.

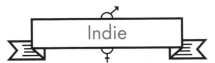

Indie

The perfect name for your future companion to any fringe festival.

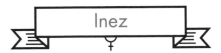

Inez

This one's layered. Like an onion. It's the Americanised spelling of the Spanish name for the Greek word *hagne*, which means 'chaste' or 'sacred'. Whew, that was confusing. But any name that takes a while to explain is sure to come in handy at social events.

Insta

What can we say? You know you want to be the first to go there. And how cute will photos of baby Insta be on your Instagram profile? #onemillionlikesaday

Ione

The name of a sea nymph in Greek mythology, this name also means 'violet flower'. Avoid if you can't say the phrase 'sea nymph' without giggling.

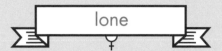

Iris

This is another old name, and it's also yet *another* flower name. Fortunately, it's also the name of the Greek goddess of the rainbow. So, you know, that's something.

Isla

A common name in Scotland, this one means 'island'. Think of the calm, the tranquillity. Just like a screaming newborn. Bonus: you can drop the 's' and still retain the correct pronunciation while making your child's name even more unique.

Ivy

More than just another botanical name, Ivy means 'faithfulness'. Ancient Greeks even used to present wreaths of ivy to newlyweds as a symbol of fidelity. So naming your girl Ivy is kind of like shoring up your relationship as well. And you know what else is groovy? Beyonce and Jay Z chose Ivy for their daughter's middle name. The baby's first name is Blue, which is on this list too, BTW. Although our spelling is edgier.

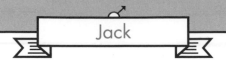

Jack

Fine. You can have this one.

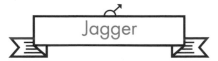

Jagger

Oh, now this one got that swagger, yo! Just pump up that terrible Maroon 5 song and your son's life is officially ruined.

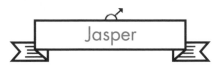

Jasper

Jasper is at once refined, playful and masculine, and it's a rarity in that it is a male gem name. There's a lot to like about this and there are some literary connections to the name as well. But, and this is a big *but*, one of those literary connections happens to be with Stephanie Meyer's *Twilight* series.

Jericho

If this isn't a soon-to-be-popular hipster name, then I don't know what is. Within the next ten years, you won't be able to say Jericho in a children's playground without turning many heads, but that might also be because you're hanging out in a children's playground saying the name Jericho to yourself.

Jezebel

In the Old Testament, Jezebel is the evil wife of a dude named Ahab (the King of Israel). She ends up being eaten by dogs. But fret not; your dachshund isn't going to eat your baby. At least, I don't think…

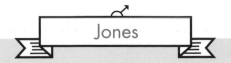

Jones

I've heard this name means 'God is gracious', but of all the common surnames-turned-first-names, there are so many more interesting options.

Jovi

This can be a boy or a girl's name. Have you ever danced to 'Livin' on a Prayer' ironically? Of course you have; it's what you do.

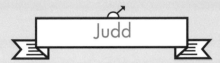

Judd

Oh, I see, you *did* spend the best part of your day queuing for a food truck. Having too much time on your hands is the hipster way, it seems. It's also a recipe for disaster on the baby naming front, too.

Julian

Robert de Niro named his son Julian – Robert *freaking* de Niro!

June

A calendar month.

Kale

He's your number-one son. Unfortunately for the world, he's also the number-one hipster. He likes pop-up stores, drinks artisan water, has a legion of followers on Instagram, where he posts pictures of the bespoke terrariums he builds, and he won't be dining out anywhere unless you can guarantee his deconstructed tofu burger will be smeared on a wooden board.

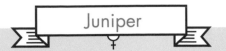

Juniper

The shrub and berry with definite hipster cred: it's the flavouring in gin that makes gin, well, gin.

Juno

I know the film made you cry happy tears with its sharp script and witty protagonist, but might this be a bad omen? This is one doodle that can't be undid, home-skillet.

Kai

This is a popular name in Malta, or so I'm told. But, true or not, just go with it; you love telling people irrelevant, little-known facts. It makes you seem smart.

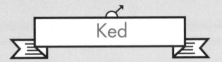

Ked

Now that you have someone to help you out with your adult colouring-in, what you may not realise is that you also have someone to join you in the ball pit they've just opened up around the corner, which is open to adults as well.

Keffiyeh

Wearing Native American war bonnets to festivals is a faux pas these days, so why not name your daughter after this symbolically significant Middle Eastern scarf instead?

Kennedy

Helpfully associated with the Kennedy family in America, this name has a regal ring to it, making it at once trendy and classic. Which is a good thing, as the name's original meanings are 'helmeted head', 'misshapen head' and/or 'ugly head'.

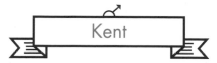

Kent

So you're angry because they haven't invented a vending machine that dispenses bike parts, but there's no reason to take it out on the lad. All little Kent wants is for you to get off your unicycle, stop grooming your beard and go and kick the ball in the park with him like a normal father would.

Kerouac

I've already ripped on his most famous work, but I'll happily do it again. The guy was overrated. That's right, you heard me, *overrated*! Stop idolising this drunk with a serious Oedipus complex – that's, like, the *worst* omen.

Kingston

A name fit for a king. Gwen Stefani chose this one for her own little lord all the way back in 2006. Does that make this one outdated?

Kinney

For the parents who want their bub to grow up to be a riot grrl. If you're expecting twins, might I suggest Sleater to complete the pair? Give that one to your least favourite, though.

Kinwa

Why not go for the phonetic spelling of your favourite grain? There's nothing more in right now, except, of course, for …

Kombucha

In keeping with food trends, this one automatically makes the grade. Little Kombi might not remind you of fermented tea, but she *was* produced from a symbiotic colony of bacteria and yeast. At least, I think that's how it happens.

Lana

Resurrected recently by Lana del Ray, who represents everything retro, glamorous, kitsch and flash-in-the-pan about hipsterdom. Them's some big shoes to fill.

Latte

Between freelance jobs, walk down to your local café with your keep cup (thank you for doing your part to save this dying planet, BTW). Take off the lid and be sure to remove your daughter before they pour in the scalding milk.

Layla

Listen to the Eric Clapton song and meditate on this name's meaning: 'night' and/or 'dark beauty'. You'll feel it, trust me.

Lena ♀

Did I mention that show *Girls*?

Lennon ♀

This one originates in Ireland and means 'lover'. Like Jagger, this name exists to commemorate a music idol.

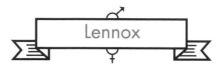

Lennox ♂♀

'Lennox, I'm coming for you' is something I hope your son or daughter never hears Mike Tyson say. But then, Lennox Lewis actually won that fight back in 2002, so … look, I just wanted to throw a sports reference in to mess with you.

Leonora ♀

Another variation on Eleanor. See Elna for my feelings about that name.

Leopold ♂

So you made it all the way through Ulysses. Congratulations! I guess you've got to make it worth your while.

Levi

With a famous brand of jeans out there, this one has kind of moved away from its biblical roots. It's got all the letters needed to spell Elvis, except the S of course, and it's only one thousand times less likely that your son will be the victim of bullying.

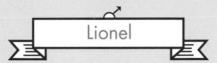

Lionel

Okay, I know we're loving some of these older names, but I'm telling you this now: Lionels rarely go on to great things.

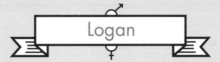

Logan

Too boyish? Well, not in the 1990s it wasn't, and with the revival of all things nineties, so too should Logan be reclaimed … by the girls.

Loki

Generally perceived to have negative connotations given its roots in Norse mythology, Loki is one of those names dying for the hipster cred that turns things round. That same touch that transforms edgy, working-class suburbs into gentrified hotbeds of cool. You know, until the rent goes up so high nobody can afford to live there anymore.

Lola

The Kinks have immortalised this name, which is a diminutive of Dolores, don't you know?

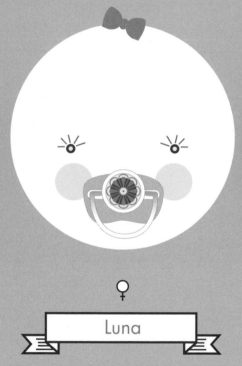

♀

Luna

It means 'moon' and makes appearances as
character names in *Harry Potter* and *True Blood*.
It's the kind of quirky name that guarantees
academic success. Don't ask me why, but I can
just imagine little Luna putting in those hours
at the library.

Lotte

While munching on wasabi peas and drinking too much craft beer, you might've come to the belief that Lotte could make an excellent name for a baby boy. But you were drunk then and hopefully sober now, so you've come to understand that this is a terrible idea and one of many reasons this book should be burnt.

Luca

Colin Firth, Vincent d'Onofrio, Hilary Duff, Rebecca Minkoff and Jacinda Barrett all don't believe Luca is too girly for a boy. But they'd all be wrong.

Lulu

This one might call to mind London's swinging sixties, where I can't imagine a go-go dancer that ever existed who wasn't named Lulu. Just make sure you've got the polka-dot minis and platform boots at the ready.

Lyla

There's a thousand interpretations for what in the heck Lyla actually means, but my personal favourite has to be that it's an acronym for 'Love You Lots Always'. Just don't count on the 'always' part, Mum and Dad.

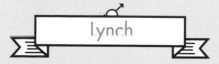

lynch

Okay, you've just gone nuts with the whole *Twin Peaks* thing, haven't you? I know the man is the original hipster, but calm yourself.

Mabel

Derived from Latin, Mabel means 'lovable' or 'dear'. 'Nuff said.

Mae

Like a lot of these old-fashioned names, Mae brings some old-world charm. Think antique. And antiques are not just chintzy crap; they're expensive, too.

Magnolia

This one presents a lot of versatility in the nickname department. Noa, Nola, Nollie and Maggie are all cute abbreviations, but I'd be just as happy if this name is a simple salute to director Paul Thomas Anderson. You can't call your baby Punch Drunk Love, after all. Although, you could try Boogie.

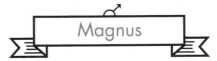

Magnus

With your ultra-PC lefty leanings, surely this one's a bit too violent. Magnus is a screaming war general who cuts an imposing figure, not a liberal arts college graduate and part-time lute player.

Maja

All I hear is Austin Powers saying this name through his horse teeth. If you can get past this image, then go right ahead. *Maja, baby!*

Major

Surprisingly less violent and threatening than Magnus opposite, Major is the perfect name for anyone who has never read Joseph Heller's satirical masterpiece, *Catch-22*. Some smart bully will cotton on eventually, though, I'm sure. *Yes, sir, Major Major Major Major!*

Mamie

Meryl Streep may call her daughter Mamie, but you know this isn't a real name. But, then, isn't that the idea?

Maple

As sweet as syrup, this one evokes images of trees thick with beautiful auburn leaves. Get back to nature.

Marmite

Okay, so I'm going to hold your hand on this one and try to walk you through it. The answer is no, first of all. But here's why: Marmite is a sticky, brown food paste made from yeast extract that tastes essentially like spreadable salt. We don't name our children after foodstuffs and we don't name our children after the kinds of foodstuffs that make a lot of people want to barf.

Mason

He's a stone worker, or at least he used to be. But I'm sure your over-educated and suitably under-employed middle-class gem will never have to don the hard hat.

Matilda

This has got to be the ultimate little girl's name, doesn't it? Forever immortalised by children's author Roald Dahl, Matilda has got to be on the list when considering your options.

Matteo

Ricky Martin, Colin Firth and Benjamin Bratt all have sons called Matteo. It's a flexible one that can be shortened to Matt, but which can also nod to your Italian or Spanish heritage depending on how many Ts you opt for.

Miller

Another common surname creeping onto first name lists, this one ensures your son will grow up to frequent drinking venues set up in the locations of disused businesses – a bar in a former public toilet, a coffee shop in what used to be a laundromat. You know, that kind of thing.

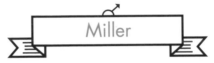

Millie

She's going to grow up to drink gin in the sunshine and, to be honest, this might just be how it all ends for Millie. But there'll be some innocent moments, too, and you'll look every bit the part of number-one parent as you yell this name across a playground while sipping on some single-origin.

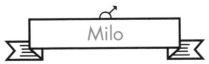

Milo

Commonly a name reserved for cats, Milo might just grow up to be a taco-loving douchebag one day. Like father, like son.

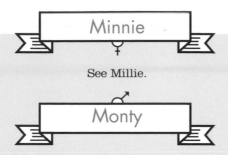

Minnie

See Millie.

Monty

Yes, poor little Monty. He grew up in a house where the sound of a ukulele wasn't considered an irritant, was handfed artisanal pickles from the time he could eat proper food, and went on to cultivate his first moustache at the age of eleven. Still, it beats having your dad lock you in the car on hot days while he got drunk in the casino. Not that I know anything about that, mind you...

Morganic

So you know a thing or two about permaculture, but do you want to perma-ruin somebody's life? I think all those foraged foods and kale chips have soiled (get it? Like, the soil, as in the earth, from which crops grow) your brain.

Moses

Now here's a pop culture reference for you. I mean, he was kind of like the first superhero, in a way. I can see him teaming up with the Avengers, parting large bodies of water for Iron Man to fly through. What? Disrespectful?

Murray

This could potentially be a unisex name. It originates from Scotland and means 'from the land by the sea'.

Nico

'It's a boy!' they exclaimed, confused as to why
you named your son after a famous female singer.
Okay, so this one is technically gender neutral, but
you do own a lot of Velvet Underground records.

Neville

What is this? A pre-emptive strike against bullying? Because it won't work, you know.

Nola

This could be the short form of Magnolia or the Gaelic name Fionnuala (which you could also abbreviate to Finn). There's something light and airy about Nola, as well as something sensual, too. But then, maybe I'm just thinking of Scarlett Jo's portrayal of Nola Rice in Woody Allen's *Match Point*.

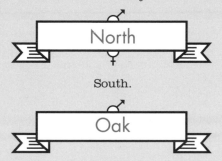

North

South.

Oak

Only the other day someone on the Internet was saying that if they chose this name their extended family would cut them off. I can't get enough of the real-life drama that crops up online, so I just hope you go with this one. Maybe I'll be reading about your dilemmas in the months to come. Fingers crossed.

Ocarina

So you've either named your daughter after a small wind instrument or because you spent far too much time playing *The Legend of Zelda* series; either way, you're a bad person.

Odessa

Your daughter is not a port city in Ukraine, and unless she's born with a ten-gallon hat on her head that makes you think instantly of Texas, I can't imagine why or how you expect this to work.

Odette

Feel like flexing those muscles of sophistication? Then try this one on for size. Odette is the White Swan, the heroine of Tchaikovsky's ballet *Swan Lake*. More recently a similar role gained actress Natalie Portman an Oscar for her portrayal of The Swan Queen in the Darren Aronofsky film *Black Swan*, a movie you no doubt saw, loved and reviewed on your blog.

Olive

There's something understated about Olive that makes for a charming first name. What else can I say? I like this one.

Oprah

Too soon, folks. This one is too soon.

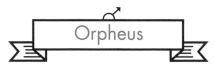

Orpheus

In Greek mythology, Orpheus was a great musician. So great, in fact, that he could literally move mountains. Rivers would stop to listen to him jamming on his lyre and trees would dance to his tunes. These days you need a MacBook and a copy of Logic Pro, but really that's just the instrument of our times. Little Orphie is destined for big things, I'm sure.

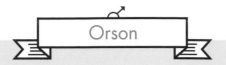

Tell us more about your days at film school. Please, we're dying to know. Actually, hang on a minute, I think I'd prefer to eat glass.

So you studied theatre in high school, got good grades, then went on to hone your craft at a dramatic arts academy. But you never got those callbacks, never booked that role. For a while you scraped by with commercial work. The pay was good, but the work only came in dribs and drabs. Then you called it quits and moved on. Now you know what's really important: creating life, being a parent! Whatever gets you through the days, dude.

Does anyone remember that absolutely bizarro kids' film from 1986 called *The Adventures of Milo and Otis*? I mean, what the hell was that? A live-action adventure/comedy/drama about a cat and a dog ...? I can't even.

You wouldn't think it to read it, but this name actually means 'riches' or 'wealth'. It's not a popular name, so you might as well start the trend before somebody else does.

As with Homer, I think we're starting to get past *Simpsons* relevance on this one, so I don't see any Otto Mann jokes coming your son's way.

Pabst

Sure, it's the name of your fave cheap American lager to drink ironically, but there's also something wholesome in the name, don't you think? Can't you just imagine little Pabst in his overalls, hay hanging out his mouth, that concerned look on his face as he comes to the realisation that the foreclosure is inevitable, that this year's crop is worthless, that the best option is to drive his car headlong into a tree. Wow, that got really dark.

Paloma

This one means 'dove' (well, technically it means 'pigeon', but you're not going to be running around telling people that, are you?). Soft yet distinct, Paloma is the favoured name of Picasso's daughter.

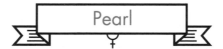

Pandora

So what if this name derives from a mythological woman who unleashes all of the evils upon the world? Get over it. This is another one of those names that needs reclaiming. And being the centre of attention wouldn't be so bad either, would it?

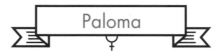

Pearl

They make jewellery out of this stuff. Classy!

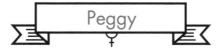

Peggy

Here's the reason to choose this name: David Lynch. You're a hipster, so you've watched every episode of *Twin Peaks*, right? Well, Peggy Lipton is the name of the actress who played Norma Jennings on that show. Also: *Mad Men*.

Phoebe

This one means 'radiant', 'shining' and, in some interpretations, 'brilliant'. All the things your Phoebe will grow up to be.

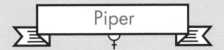

Piper

You've lost some hours watching *Orange is the New Black* recently, so give back a little. Alternatively, you could always just name your daughter Netflix.

Pixar

This is sort of the inverse of the last one. Maybe watch some Pixar movies and allow *them* to inspire the name choice ...?

Polaroid

Nothing says retro quite like this, and it reflects your favourite hobby: taking selfies. Sorry, I meant 'photography'.

Poppy

If you're fortunate enough to have seen Mike Leigh's comedy-drama *Happy-Go-Lucky* then you've found a character worthy of inspiring this name choice. While not a hallmark of movie pop culture, the role did garner a Golden Globe Award and a Silver Bear for actress Sally Hawkins. It's on Netflix right now, so do yourself a favour.

♀

Prius

The hybrid car that was created as an innovative solution to our global environmental crisis, this is one for you forward-thinkers and global warming–haters.

Potter

Yes, we've established that surnames are in, but so long as YA novels about wizards are too, this one just has to stay off your list.

Prairie

If you're American, then this name might carry a hint of patriotism with it. But that's neither here nor there for the rest of you. Prairie remains a terribly uncommon nature name and makes a great alternative to names like Meadow and Autumn, and more modern Ps such as Promise or Praise.

Prue

Typically short for Prudence, this is another 'Do we put the nickname on the birth certificate?' scenario. The choice is yours, but there's no going back once you commit.

Pythagoras

How will you ever explain this to anyone? But then, maybe you're just jonesing for an excuse to bust out that abacus you've never used. You know, in the name of all things retro. Word of advice, however, children trust their parents implicitly – they have to. You might be getting off on the wrong foot here.

Quince

My favourite paste when eating cheese, she's bound to go down just as well while entertaining.

Rae

The feminine version of Ray, this one looks as bad as it sounds. Why not slot a 'v' between the 'a' and 'e' and relive those memories of taking ecstasy. Hey, that sentence rhymes!

Raina

Water falling from the sky. F@#$ing A!

Raven

The Poe fans have probably gone straight for this one, giving off an edgy, gothic vibe and calling to mind Tim Burton's cinematic oeuvre. And, like Burton, the name Raven peaked in the 1990s, but we've got our fingers crossed for that comeback.

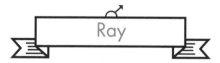
Ray

He makes home brew. It's what he does.

Rebel

Shouting this one out loud might be a tad embarrassing, but it's up to you in the end. But seriously, just picture a grown man or woman shouting this name in anger the day Rebel actually rebels. Good for you irony-lovers, I suppose.

Ripley

The strong, practical-minded heroine of Ridley Scott's *Alien*, this is a great strong female character for a girl to idolise. It's also a perfect name for a pet. Or a child.

Robinson

This one has some strong literary connections, conjuring up imagery of craggy rocks and deserted islands. Both *Robinson Crusoe* and *The Swiss Family Robinson* are tales of survival, which bodes well for a young man setting out in life.

Roman

Sure, Polanski made some classic films, but don't let that semester-long course on film noir dictate a major life choice here. The director of *Chinatown* had … a few foibles, let's say.

Romily

This one has a long history dating back to the Romans. It has predominantly been a male name, but recent trends see it being given more commonly to females. That being said, this name is not at all *common*; it's a rare one that possesses the daintiness typically reserved for flower names – only minus the stupid flowers.

Romy

If you don't spend your evenings hanging about old theatres that play ancient, subtitled, European black-and-white features, then you may not know a thing about Romy Schneider. If that's the case, then you're no hipster: you're just a fake.

The most masculine of them all. Just go to Urban Dictionary. Go on, whip your iPhone out. I'll wait.

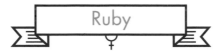

You're probably thinking this one is too obvious. Well, it kind of is. Not only is Ruby the name of a red gemstone, but it's peaking in popularity right now. But don't let that stop you, because surely you're not letting trends dictate your daughter's future. What kind of person would that make you?

Why not name your child after Santa's most well-known reindeer? Or you could always, like, not do that.

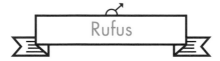

Be honest: how many times have you seen Mr Wainwright in concert? I once shared a drink with the man in a bar in Manhattan many years ago. Strange things will happen while drinking alone in New York – but that's a story for another time. Did you know that Rufus is synonymous with red-headedness? Yuck, you say? Well, I'm a redhead too, so take *that*! But yeah, it sucks.

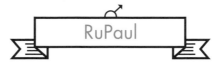

I see glitter and shoulder pads and disco balls in his future.

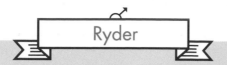

Ryder

Meaning 'cavalryman' and/or 'messenger', Ryder also carries with it a subtle literary reference, being the surname of *Brideshead Revisited* protagonist Charles Ryder. And surnames turned into first names are totes in these days!

Sadie

She's too young to be thought of as sexy, so ignore the Beatles' song for now, but what Sadie really means is 'princess', which is much more age-appropriate.

Salinger

Unlike Ryder, this ain't subtle. But hey, who cares, we need to know how well-read you are. (You realise everyone has read that book, don't you? We got forced to in high school.)

Sanford

This is a strong, masculine-sounding first name. It pretty much guarantees your boy will grow up to play squash, attend board meetings and end up with an enormous investment portfolio and a rap sheet for embezzlement. I mean, I'm not sure how exactly, but it will.

Scout

If your boyfriend dresses like a lumberjack in winter but doesn't have the muscle to lift a twig, then this unisex name has to be on your list of possibilities.

Seven

Well, it's got George Costanza's approval.
That's something, I guess.

Sebastian

Here's a rarity: a decent, honest-to-god, *real* name, meaning 'venerable' and 'revered'. Pair it up with Viola for a Shakespearean feel if you must, I don't even care. Seb makes for an awesome nickname, too. You have my blessing.

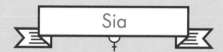

Sia

Do you like odd Australian musicians who sing songs about light fittings?
Of course you do.

Simone

Simone is the French, feminine version of Simon, and you've got two über-cool ladies to select as a namesake for your daughter: philosopher Simone de Beauvoir and musician/activist Nina Simone. Kinda ticking all the boxes, right?

Snow

River, Rain, Summer, Liberty and Joaquin were the names of the Phoenix kids, so whether you want your child to win an Oscar or OD at The Viper Room, this name's got you covered. Pass on that torch to the next generation.

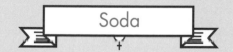

Soda

I'm thinking Stream for the middle name.

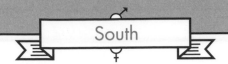

South

Which direction will I take this one in? Haha. Get it? You should, because you're about to become a parent, and these jokes will soon be your bread and butter.

Soy

This one was bound to pop up, wasn't it? Just like the milk you insist on drinking, your precious bundle of joy is going to one day drive us all to distraction. But you don't care, do you? It's your lifestyle. Your choice.

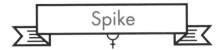

Spike

Now, come on. We all loved *The Land Before Time*, but this just isn't suitable for a young lady.

Stella

'Hey, Stella! Hey, Stella!' Stop screaming at that Belgian pilsner you're holding. You've had enough to drink.

Stellan

'Hey, Stellan! Hey, Stellan!'

Stevie ♀

If you Fleetwood Mac fans don't want to be too transparent, then Stevie is another option. It's still a proclamation of your music tastes, and also adds a splash of tomboy to the mix, breaking down those gender barriers.

♂ Sullivan

This is one hell of a strong, masculine name. It screams words like moustache and aviator, and you've got to love Sully for a nickname. A perfect name if you want your son to end up like good old Sully Sullenberger, who landed a freaking plane on the Hudson freaking River! Now that's butch!

Sybil ♀

Popular culture hasn't been kind to Sybil over the years: Basil Fawlty's long-suffering wife was called Sybil, as was the character with multiple personalities in the book of the same name. But Sybil actually means 'prophetess'. Not so tragic, after all.

♂ Talin

Kind of like the claw, only spelled differently. Edgy, I guess.

Tallulah ♀

It's easy on the ear and means 'leaping water', so I'm told. Tallulah was born to attend weekend-long music festivals and wear strapless maxis while lounging in the sun.

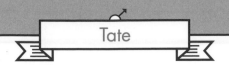

Tate

What says 'culture' like naming your son after an art gallery? Nothing, that's what. Don't ask us, just ask Baby Spice. She named her second son Tate and she's way hipper than any of us, right?

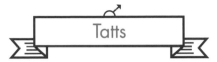

Tatts

How could we go past this one? Have you spent your twenties adorning yourself in regrettable ink stains? Well, they're permanent, just like your son's name will be an everlasting source of torment and shame.

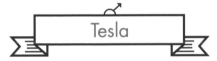

Tesla

Sure, you know it's the surname of a scientist, but nowadays it's the brand name of an electric car as well. Innovative is the word. He will pick on his little sister, Prius.

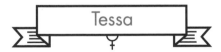

Tessa

Surely this one is too common for you. It's already gained status as an independent first name, moving away from its original position as the short form of Theresa.

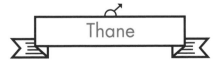

Thane

From the Old English meaning 'one who serves', and familiar to our ears thanks to Shakespeare's *Macbeth*, Thane presents an opportunity to at once tick the culture box and move away from dated Zane or Wayne.

Theo

Short for Theodore, Theo has been taking off as an independent first name in recent years. It's popular in a handful of European countries right now, so jump on the bandwagon; we all know how sophisticated them Europeans are.

Thor

Most people these days would associate this name with the caped comic-book crusader played by an Aussie with a top-notch bod, rather than the Norse god of thunder. Don't let your man-crush rule your decision.

Tidal

At this point, if you've read this far, just do whatever the hell you want.

Tierney

For crying out loud, who comes up with this stuff?

Tulle

So you spent the day on Pinterest getting inspiration for your next craft project. Now you're thinking about naming your child after a lightweight material. Time to shut the MacBook Air and switch your brain back on.

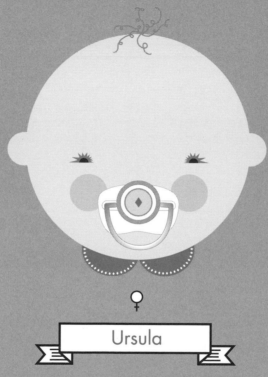

Ursula

She scared the pants off you when you were a kid watching Disney's *The Little Mermaid*. And if that's not enough nostalgia to get you frothing at the mouth, then the original Bond girl, Honey Ryder, was played by none other than Ursula Andress (which honestly sounds like a Bond girl name in and of itself).

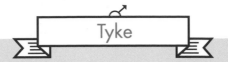

Tyke

This one seems a little offensive, no? But then, that's what we like, a bit of controversy. Shouting this one across a playground could end in your arrest, so just be sure to carry that birth certificate with you at all times.

Valencia

Meaning 'brave' or 'strong', this is a good one, should you not only want a daughter but a bodyguard as well.

Van

Plenty of culture cred in this one, and everybody knows those monosyllabic names are the funkiest. Plus, vans are carrier vehicles. They help move things. That's useful.

Velma

So long as Hollywood doesn't decide to reboot Scooby Doo *again*, we're far enough away from the orange turtleneck-clad character now for your daughter to avoid the comparison on the playground – so long as her peers don't have Cartoon Network.

Vera

Another name that evokes old-world charm, this name peaked in popularity in the 1910s. It also has a connection to Alfred Hitchcock's 1960 masterpiece, *Psycho*, where Vera Miles was the actress who played Marion Crane's sister.

Viola

The name of a Shakespearean character *and* a musical instrument. That's highbrow!

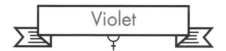

Violet

Like many of the names gaining traction today, this is one of those ones that was popular a very long time ago. But with people like Ben Affleck and Jennifer Garner naming their first daughter Violet, it has the celeb cred needed for a revival. Let's just hope Ben and Jen can work things out.

Waldo

If you reside in the US or Canada, then you might be a bit hesitant to use this one. Waldo, of course, was the name of the white-and-red-striped man hidden away in all of those Martin Handford illustrations (he was named Wally, as in *Where's Wally?*, everywhere else). But surely we've gotten past that now, and with your eBay alert set to reclaim everything from your childhood, who knows? Maybe there's just the right amount of nostalgia in this name for you to reclaim it, too.

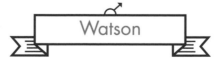

Watson

I went to school with a boy called Watson. He smoked *a lot* of pot. But that's my life, not yours. I'm pretty sure it had nothing to do with his name anyway.

Wayfare

Do you love reminiscing about the 1980s, a decade you were most likely born in, but never got to experience? Yes? Well, this is perfect then.

Wentworth

So, apparently, Wentworth means 'village of the white people'. So ... ah ... yeah ...

Wes

Somewhere between watching *The Royal Tenenbaums* over and over and listening to your Elliott Smith CDs, you've found time to procreate. Lucky us.

Willa

Another name with plenty of celeb cred, Willa has been chosen by Keri Russell, David Mamet, Brian de Palma and the late Philip Seymour Hoffman. Additionally, this name conjures up the image of a willow tree with all its ghostly beauty.

Williamsburg

The only name on this list that can compete with the hipster cred of naming your son Brooklyn.

Wilma

If you're unlucky, your only memory of the *Flintstones* was that disastrous live-action movie starring John Goodman and Rick Moranis. Otherwise you might be able to start with a clean slate and breathe new life into an old name that's been dead as a dodo since the hugely successful Hanna-Barbera cartoon killed it in the 1960s.

Winona

Before she started making cutesy indie flicks and shoplifting, she stormed around your living room throwing tantrums in ballet flats. Ah, memories.

Winston

Another one of the names in here that calls to mind a past era. There's not a more famous namesake than Mr Churchill, who is quoted as having said this: 'Success consists of going from failure to failure without loss of enthusiasm.' That seems kind of pertinent right now, doesn't it?

Wisky

It's what you imbibed while penning your first manuscript, but while the literary career never went anywhere and you gave up the bottle when you realised your father would never apologise (not in any real, meaningful way), you can still keep the name of your first love alive. Okay, that one got a little too real for me.

Wolfgang

Do you know the meaning of the word 'ostentatious'? Look it up.

Woodstock

Oh, yes, you're all about nostalgia, aren't you? As a cynic, I'm prone to thinking this moment in history was probably little more than a big group of people getting drunk in a park and listening to music, but with the gloss of time passing, Woodstock has become synonymous with all the positivity that the counterculture had to offer. Shine on, you crazy diamond.

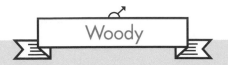

Woody

He's the lovable sheriff from the *Toy Story* films. He's that charismatic Texan actor with the goofy big grin. And he's the famous *let's-not-talk-about-his-questionable-personal-life-because-he's-still-making-good-movies* New York director who has been churning out screwball dramedies since the Stone Age. He's Woody.

Wren

Yes, it's the name of a small, muddy-brown bird from the unfortunately named *Troglodytidae* family, but hey, it sounds cute.

Xena

I actually named my childhood guinea pig after the Warrior Princess. She died after I overfed her and left her outside for too long on a hot summer's day. Protip: don't do this to your child.

Xiomara

I honestly don't know what to say at this point.

Yara

I'm giving this one a pass. It's a fun alternative to Mara, Sara or Lara and means a multitude of things across the globe. In Brazil, Yara can mean 'forest girl' or 'water witch', while in Greek it can mean 'the loved one'. The Arabic translations are best of all, however: 'precious ruby' or, my favourite, 'romantic music under the moon'.

Zane

All I can think of is actor Billy Zane and his career kind of went nowhere. So, good luck with that.

Zeitgeist

Your child may come to define the spirit of their time. This name choice might just come to define the spirit of ours. This one means 'time ghost' in German, perhaps a nod to the time spent getting your culture on in Berlin?

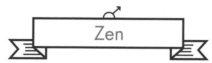

Zelda

At some point somebody will commit suicide after she leaves them. Just saying.

Zen

Yeah, you're feeling the irony of this one, aren't you? Supress those murderous impulses born from lack of sleep and your complete, total and utter exhaustion, and repeat that mantra one more time. Baby Zen – he's so sweet with all his crying and shitting.

Zephyr

I'll give this one a pass, because we're almost done. It's a classic with all kinds of meanings, evoking all manner of images and emotions. Zephyr. I like it.

Ziggy

She's hip, she's fly, she's all of the outdated terms I know for 'cool', but for goodness sake she better learn a musical instrument or this will be a failed experiment.

Zinnia

Sure, technically this is another flower name, but have you ever heard it before? Okay, maybe you did when you were playing Pokemon.

Zola

Seeing as Balzac doesn't appear in this book, why not try Zola? With its African roots (it means 'tranquil' in Zulu) and literary connections, this one definitely makes a statement.

Zooey

Congratulations, you've just given birth to another manic pixie dream girl. You know, that weird yet oddly attractive girl who will go on to embolden a stream of broodingly soulful young men to embrace life and take action. You ought to know, she's your daughter.

Zowie

No guarantees this one will stick. Your boy might just end up calling himself Duncan Jones instead. How dull. But that's parenting, folks. All you can do is try and hope for the best.

Published in 2016 by Smith Street Books
Melbourne | Australia
smithstreetbooks.com

ISBN: 978-1-925418-24-8

Publisher: Paul McNally
Design and illustration concept: Michelle Mackintosh
Design and illustrations: Heather Menzies

Printed & bound in China by C&C Offset Printing Co., Ltd.

Book 6
10 9 8 7 6 5 4 3 2